Navigating Open Source's Networked Nuances

A Comprehensive Overview of Open Source Software Licensing

Grace Hendricks

Table of Contents

1 Introduction to Open Source

Open source software (OSS) fundamentally alters the traditional software development paradigm. Unlike proprietary software, where source code remains hidden and controlled by a single entity, OSS makes the source code publicly available. This transparency fosters collaboration, allowing developers worldwide to contribute, modify, and distribute the software. This shared ownership model not only speeds up development but also enhances the software's quality through collective scrutiny and improvement. The collaborative nature of OSS stands in stark contrast to the often isolated environment of proprietary software development.

This shared access to the source code is only one piece of the puzzle. The ethos of open source goes far beyond simply making code available; it's about a collaborative spirit, driven by the belief that shared knowledge benefits all. Transparency isn't merely a feature; it's a fundamental principle, fostering trust and accountability. This community-driven approach often leads to faster innovation and quicker adaptation to user needs, resulting in more robust and adaptable software than is typically seen in closed-source development. Consider the Linux kernel, a shining example of the power of collaborative open source development, powering countless servers and devices globally.

Understanding the implications of open source licenses is crucial. Licenses dictate the terms of use, distribution, and modification of the software. Choosing the wrong license can have significant legal and commercial consequences. A license that is too restrictive could stifle innovation, while one that is too permissive might not offer sufficient protection to the original developers. The consequences of noncompliance can be severe, ranging from legal action to reputational damage. Therefore, understanding the nuances of various licenses is critical for both developers and users. The choice of license isn't just a technical detail; it's a fundamental aspect of project governance.

Several key licenses define the landscape of open-source software. The GNU General Public License (GPL), for example, is a copyleft license requiring that any derivative works remain under the same license, ensuring that the modified code remains open source. In contrast, the permissive MIT license allows for more freedom, permitting modifications and redistribution even in proprietary projects, providing developers with flexibility but perhaps less community control. Choosing between copyleft and permissive licenses depends on the goals of the project and the desired level of community involvement. It's a decision that needs careful consideration, weighing the benefits of shared development against the potential drawbacks of constraints on commercial use.

Navigating the legal complexities surrounding OSS can be challenging. Copyright, a cornerstone of intellectual property, protects the original code, while the license itself dictates the permitted uses of that code. Attribution, a common requirement in many licenses, ensures proper credit to the original authors. Patent issues can also arise, as open-source projects might inadvertently infringe on existing patents. Addressing these legal aspects is not simply a matter of compliance; it's essential for fostering trust and collaboration within the open-source community. The very success of the open-source movement relies upon a clear understanding and responsible application of intellectual property rights.

Beyond the legal frameworks, open-source communities are the driving force behind the success of many projects. These communities, often dispersed geographically, operate through collaborative platforms, fostering communication and information sharing. Effective governance is key to maintaining order and promoting efficiency within these diverse groups. Models range from loosely structured communities to those with formal structures and elected leaders. Contributing to an open-source project can be a rewarding experience, offering opportunities to learn from other developers and collaborate on cutting-edge technologies. Understanding the dynamics of these communities, from communication styles to decision-making processes, is crucial for effective participation.

Open source is not solely a philanthropic endeavor; it holds significant commercial implications. Many companies utilize open-source software to reduce development costs, leverage existing codebases, and tap into a vast pool of contributors. However, successfully monetizing an open-source project requires a strategic approach, potentially involving offering commercial support, customization services, or premium features to users. This commercial viability demonstrates that open source can be a sustainable and economically successful model, showing that sharing doesn't always equate to a loss of revenue. The choice of business model will naturally depend on the specific context and goals of the project.

The future of open source licensing promises exciting possibilities but also poses considerable challenges. Emerging trends such as the increasing use of AI in software development, may raise new questions regarding copyright and licensing. Ethical considerations surrounding data usage and privacy will continue to shape the evolution of open-source practices. Navigating these developments requires proactive engagement and a commitment to fostering responsible and sustainable open-source ecosystems. Open source, far from being a static entity, is a dynamic and continuously evolving landscape that needs constant attention and adaptation.

1.1 Defining Open Source

Open source, at its core, signifies software with source code made publicly accessible, permitting users not only to utilize the software but also to examine, modify, and redistribute it, often with certain conditions. This accessibility fosters a collaborative environment, unlike the closed nature of proprietary software, where source code remains hidden, restricting modification and redistribution to the copyright holder. This fundamental difference shapes the entire ecosystem and its possibilities.

The defining characteristic, however, isn't just the availability of the source code; it's the accompanying license. These licenses, which vary considerably, dictate the terms under which the software can be used, modified, and shared. They establish the boundaries of permitted actions, ensuring a balance between allowing open collaboration and safeguarding the rights of creators. Understanding these licenses is crucial, as using open-source software incorrectly can lead to legal complications.

Think of it as a shared recipe. A proprietary recipe is kept secret, only the chef can make the dish. An open-source recipe, however, is available for everyone to view, adapt, and even sell. But some open-source recipes may require attribution – you need to mention the original chef – or forbid commercial use. The license explains the “rules” of sharing and adapting this recipe. Neglecting these rules can lead to misunderstandings or even lawsuits. The license clarifies these terms of use.

The open-source model thrives on community participation. This collaborative approach frequently leads to faster development cycles, improved software quality through collective code review, and a wide range of applications tailored to different needs. This decentralized, bottom-up innovation contrasts sharply with the centralized development model common in proprietary software. The benefits of community-driven development extend beyond bug fixes and feature enhancements; it fosters a shared sense of ownership and responsibility within the project. This inherent collaborative spirit often results in software that is more robust, adaptable, and ultimately, more valuable.

It's important to distinguish between open-source and free software. While many open-source projects are free of charge, the term "open source" primarily refers to the accessibility and freedom to modify the source code, not necessarily its cost. A project might be open source but require payment for support or additional features; conversely, free software doesn't automatically imply open source, as some free software might have restricted access to the source code. This distinction avoids potential confusions regarding the actual implications of choosing an open-source solution over a proprietary one. Therefore, careful consideration should be given to the specifics of both open-source and free software licensing to ensure proper understanding and usage.

The rise of open source significantly impacts software development methodologies and collaborative practices. This shift towards collaborative models has transformed not only the technical aspects of software creation but also the cultural landscape of software engineering. The very act of contributing to open-source projects is a testament to this collaborative model, encouraging a more transparent and open approach to problem-solving and product development. It represents a significant paradigm shift from proprietary development models that emphasize secrecy and control. The collaborative aspect creates a diverse pool of expertise and encourages continuous improvement.

Navigating the nuances of open-source licensing can feel like navigating a minefield, particularly for those unfamiliar with legal terminology and intellectual property rights. However, understanding the basics—the key differences between permissive licenses (like MIT) and copyleft licenses (like GPL)—is the first step toward safe and compliant use of open-source software. Familiarizing oneself with the specific terms and conditions of each license before incorporating any open-source component into a project is essential to avoid legal pitfalls and ensure smooth usage. Ignoring this crucial aspect can have serious consequences, leading to potential legal disputes and project disruptions.

Open source is not simply a technological phenomenon; it's a socio-economic movement that has profoundly impacted the software industry and beyond. The open-source model promotes transparency, collaboration, and community-driven development, fostering innovation and improving software quality. It is a testament to the power of collective intelligence and shared knowledge, reshaping how software is developed, distributed, and utilized across various sectors. The open-source ecosystem is a vibrant and dynamic landscape, continuously evolving and expanding its influence on technological advancements and societal progress. Moreover, the long-term effects on the development and dissemination of technology continue to be felt globally.

1.2 The Open Source Philosophy

The open-source philosophy isn't merely a set of rules; it's a deeply held belief in the power of collaboration and shared knowledge. At its core, it champions the idea that software should be freely accessible, modifiable, and distributable, fostering a spirit of community and innovation far beyond the capabilities of proprietary models. This isn't just about altruism, though; the inherent benefits are substantial, driving faster development cycles, increased security through collective scrutiny, and a more adaptable and robust software ecosystem. The inherent flexibility allows projects to evolve quickly, adapting to user needs and technological advances in ways that are often impossible with closed-source alternatives. The result is software that is not only better but also more resilient and responsive to the ever-changing demands of the digital landscape.

Think about the sheer volume of collective intelligence harnessed in an open-source project. Hundreds, even thousands, of developers from around the world may contribute their expertise, catching bugs, suggesting improvements, and adding features that would take a single company years to implement. This collaborative environment breeds innovation in ways that closed systems simply cannot replicate. The collective expertise results in faster bug fixing, quicker responses to security vulnerabilities, and a constant stream of improvements that greatly benefit all users, ensuring the software's longevity and continual relevance. The open nature of the process reduces risk and increases reliability, building trust among users and encouraging wider adoption. This increased user base, in turn, leads to more feedback and contributions, furthering the cycle of improvement and innovation.

However, the open-source philosophy is more than just technical collaboration. It fundamentally shifts the power dynamic. Instead of a single entity controlling the software's destiny, control is decentralized amongst the community. This empowers individuals and smaller organizations who might otherwise lack the resources to compete with larger corporations. This democratizing aspect allows for a fairer and more inclusive technological landscape. It levels the playing field for smaller teams, startups, and independent developers, fostering competition and innovation through increased participation. Moreover, open access fosters transparency, allowing users to understand the software's inner workings and making it easier to identify and address potential security vulnerabilities. This transparency is a crucial component of building trust and confidence in the software.

The philosophy extends beyond code itself. Open-source projects often embrace open communication and transparent development processes. This fosters a strong sense of community, building trust and encouraging ongoing participation. Discussions, bug reports, and feature requests are publicly accessible, creating a dynamic feedback loop that improves the software and fosters a deeper understanding of the project's goals and direction. The open nature of communication builds a stronger relationship between developers and users, resulting in a product that more closely aligns with the users' requirements.

This approach, however, doesn't come without its challenges. Coordinating a diverse group of contributors requires strong leadership and clear communication. Managing contributions, resolving conflicts, and ensuring code quality demand effective organizational structures and a collaborative spirit. Navigating these challenges is critical to the project's success and requires a proactive and well-structured approach to conflict resolution and contribution management. The importance of effective communication and conflict resolution cannot be overstated. Without a robust process, open-source projects can become fractured and unproductive.

Furthermore, the reliance on volunteer contributions can be unpredictable. Maintaining consistent progress and ensuring timely releases requires careful planning and effective community engagement. This necessitates building a vibrant, active community around the project and cultivating a culture of ongoing participation and contribution.

Strategies for engaging new contributors, and strategies for retaining experienced members, are critical for the project's long-term viability. Without a dedication to cultivating a thriving community, the project risks stagnation and eventual decline.

Despite these challenges, the open-source philosophy remains a powerful force shaping the software landscape. It represents a paradigm shift towards collaboration, transparency, and community-driven development. It empowers individuals, fosters innovation, and ultimately leads to better, more reliable, and more secure software. Its ongoing evolution reflects the inherent adaptability and resilience of the open-source approach, proving its capacity to adapt to the ever-changing challenges of the technology sector. The continued growth and impact of open-source software demonstrate the strength and potential of this unique and enduring philosophy. The open-source philosophy, therefore, is not just a technical approach but a social and ethical commitment to shared knowledge and collaborative progress.

2 Major Open Source Licenses

Understanding the nuances of open-source licenses is crucial for both developers and users. Each license dictates specific rights and restrictions, impacting how you can use, modify, and distribute the software. Choosing the wrong license can lead to legal complications and hinder your project's progress. This chapter will explore some of the most prominent licenses, helping you understand their core features.

The GNU General Public License (GPL), in its various versions, is perhaps the most well-known. A key characteristic is its "copyleft" nature—requiring any derivative works to also be licensed under the GPL. This ensures that modifications and improvements remain open-source, fostering a collaborative environment. The GPL's strength lies in its strong protection of the software's freedoms, but it can also be restrictive for projects that aim for greater flexibility in licensing their derivatives. GPLv3, the current version, aims to address some concerns raised about earlier iterations, clarifying aspects related to digital rights management and patents. Understanding the implications of copyleft is essential for anyone working with GPL-licensed software. Choosing GPL often necessitates a certain level of community engagement and transparency which may or may not be desirable depending on one's aims.

Contrastingly, the MIT License offers a more permissive approach. It grants users broad rights to use, modify, and distribute the software, even in proprietary projects, with minimal obligations. Essentially, users only need to retain the original copyright notice. This makes the MIT License extremely popular for libraries and smaller projects where a less restrictive license is preferred. The simplicity and freedom provided by the MIT License make it attractive for developers seeking a straightforward legal framework without significant constraints on commercial use or modification. Its simplicity, however, means fewer protections for the original authors, relying more on the community and marketplace recognition to ensure its successful continuity.

The Apache License 2.0, another widely used permissive license, strikes a balance between permissive use and protection of the original author's intellectual property. While allowing modifications and distribution, it includes provisions against patent infringement claims and limits liability for the copyright holders. This license is particularly suitable for larger projects where collaborative development is crucial, as it offers a robust yet flexible legal framework to protect both contributors and users, fostering collaboration while still offering strong legal protections for its creators. This makes it a preferred choice in many large-scale open source endeavors.

The BSD licenses, including the 3-clause and 2-clause versions, are also permissive licenses with various degrees of attribution requirements. The 3-clause BSD License requires the inclusion of the original copyright and disclaimer notices, along with a specific clause about the license. The 2-clause license omits this clause, further broadening usage flexibility. This family of licenses offers developers a range of options, allowing them to choose the level of attribution they prefer depending on their specific needs and project scope, balancing the requirements of protection with the openness of collaboration. They offer a flexible middle ground between very restrictive and very open licenses.

The Mozilla Public License (MPL) and the Lesser General Public License (LGPL) represent different strategies within the open-source licensing ecosystem. The MPL is designed to balance the benefits of open-source collaboration with the needs of commercial entities. It allows for linking with proprietary software, offering a flexibility missing in more restrictive licenses like the GPL. LGPL, a variation of the GPL, is specifically designed for libraries and components. It permits linking with proprietary software, while requiring only the modified parts of the library to remain open source, unlike the GPL's requirement for the entire derived work. Both licenses offer a way to manage the interaction of open and proprietary software while still emphasizing the principles of openness and collaboration within the open source framework.

Choosing the right open-source license is a critical decision with long-term consequences for your project. A thorough understanding of these different licenses and their implications is essential to make an informed choice that aligns with your project's goals and intended use. Careful consideration of the balance between open collaboration and potential commercial exploitation is essential. Remember to consult legal professionals if you have specific questions regarding the nuances of a particular license and its application to your unique circumstances. The right license can set your project up for success, while the wrong one can impede its progress and cause significant legal headaches down the road.

2.1 GPL and its Variations

The GNU General Public License (GPL), a cornerstone of the open-source movement, ensures that any software derived from GPL-licensed code remains open. This "copyleft" approach, a crucial differentiator, mandates that modifications and derived works must also be distributed under the same license. This creates a ripple effect, fostering collaboration and preventing the enclosure of open source within proprietary systems. The strength of the GPL lies in its viral nature, ensuring the continued openness of the software ecosystem.

Understanding the GPL's implications is crucial. It's not merely about granting permission to use; it's about obligating redistribution under the same terms. This means if you incorporate GPL-licensed code into your project, your entire project, with few exceptions, must be released under the GPL as well. This can be a significant constraint for projects aiming for a more restrictive license. Weighing this restriction against the collaborative potential is key to successful GPL utilization.

Several variations exist, each with subtle nuances. The GPLv2, an older version, is still widely used, while GPLv3 attempts to address concerns related to digital rights management (DRM) and software patents. The key differences often relate to the specifics of how derivative works must be licensed and the treatment of specific technologies or practices that have evolved since the initial release of the GPL. While the core principle remains consistent—the propagation of openness—the details can significantly affect how a project can be used and shared.

GPLv3, for example, incorporates provisions aimed at preventing restrictions on the freedoms offered by the open-source license. It addresses concerns about the use of DRM and tries to explicitly preserve user freedom. This contrasts with GPLv2, which, while not explicitly endorsing DRM, lacks provisions explicitly addressing those concerns. Choosing between versions depends heavily on a project's goals and the potential risks associated with the adoption of specific technologies. Understanding these nuances is crucial for choosing the right version for your specific project needs.

The LGPL, or Lesser General Public License, presents a notable variation. Unlike the GPL, it grants greater flexibility regarding the licensing of derivative works. While modifications to the LGPL-licensed code itself must remain under the LGPL, linking the code to proprietary software is permitted, provided the resulting combined work provides the user with the same freedoms given by the LGPL. This makes the LGPL attractive for library projects, allowing for more permissive integration into commercial applications.

Consider the implications for developers and businesses. The GPL's viral nature, while beneficial for maintaining openness, can be a deterrent to commercial ventures seeking to integrate open-source components while maintaining proprietary control. They must carefully weigh the commitment to open-source principles against the need to protect their intellectual property and revenue streams. This means understanding the implications of using GPL-licensed libraries within proprietary products.

The choice between the GPL and its variations is not simply a matter of legal compliance; it's a philosophical decision about the direction and nature of your project. Do you prioritize the preservation of complete openness, even at the cost of potential limitations? Or do you value a balance between openness and control, allowing for more flexibility in integration with proprietary software? Choosing correctly requires a thorough understanding of your goals, your target audience, and the implications of each licensing option. Remember, this choice will significantly influence the trajectory and potential impact of your project.
Finally, staying updated is vital. Open-source licensing is an evolving field. New interpretations and legal challenges emerge regularly. Keeping informed about recent developments, legal precedents, and best practices is vital to ensuring ongoing compliance and avoiding potential pitfalls. Consult with legal experts, stay active in relevant open-source communities, and regularly review the licensing documents to ensure your project remains in compliance with the chosen license. This diligence will protect your project and contribute to the health of the broader open-source ecosystem. Ignoring this aspect can lead to legal issues and undermine the benefits of open source.

2.2 MIT License Explained

The MIT License, often lauded for its simplicity and permissiveness, grants recipients exceptionally broad rights. It's a short, concise license, easily understood even by those without extensive legal backgrounds. This straightforwardness makes it a favorite among developers, particularly for projects where maximum flexibility and minimal restrictions are desired. The core principle is one of generous allowance; it's designed to encourage widespread adoption and modification.
Unlike some licenses that impose reciprocal obligations, the MIT License doesn't require you to release your derivative works under the same terms. This freedom is a significant advantage for those who might want to incorporate MIT-licensed code into proprietary projects

without being bound by the conditions of the original license. This flexibility is a key reason for its popularity in commercial settings. Businesses can freely integrate MIT-licensed components into their software without fear of being constrained by open-source stipulations on their own products.

However, this permissive nature is not without its potential downsides. While the freedom it offers is attractive, it also means less protection for the original creators. There's no requirement for attribution in every instance, though many projects encourage it as a matter of courtesy and good practice. This lack of mandatory attribution could potentially lead to the loss of credit for the original developers, a concern for some who see attribution as a form of acknowledgement and recognition for their contributions. The very freedom it promotes could, ironically, diminish the recognition afforded to its creators.

The absence of a copyleft clause also presents another consideration. In simpler terms, the MIT License doesn't mandate that modifications or derivative works be released under the same license. This absence of a "copyleft" means that someone could take your code, make substantial changes, and release it under a completely different, possibly restrictive license, or even make it proprietary, benefiting commercially from your initial work without further obligation. This aspect needs careful consideration before selecting the MIT License for any project. For projects where strong community involvement or a unified licensing approach is prioritized, other options might be more suitable.

Understanding the nuances of the MIT License involves recognizing the trade-off between freedom and protection. It provides exceptional liberty for users, allowing broad integration into various projects and encouraging widespread adoption. This often makes it a practical and efficient choice for libraries, tools, or small components where broader usage is desirable and the potential risk of losing control over derivative works is acceptable. But its permissive nature could also pose challenges for developers highly invested in maintaining control over their intellectual property and ensuring their credit is maintained.

It's crucial to analyze the specific circumstances and objectives of a project. If the primary goal is to foster maximum dissemination and facilitate easy integration by others, then the MIT License could be an excellent choice. On the other hand, if maintaining control over the evolution of the software and the acknowledgment of the original authors are paramount considerations, a different license that mandates attribution or employs a copyleft clause would offer a greater degree of protection. The decision hinges on understanding and weighing these factors based on individual needs and priorities. In essence, a thorough understanding of the license's implications and the project's goals is essential.

The simplicity of the MIT License makes it easily accessible and readily comprehensible, a significant advantage for both developers and users. However, this simplicity masks the need for careful consideration of the potential consequences. While the lack of restrictive stipulations is highly attractive, the trade-off regarding control and attribution should be carefully evaluated. The ultimate success of selecting the MIT License is directly linked to understanding its implications in the context of the broader project goals. It's not a one-size-fits-all solution, and a conscious decision informed by a careful assessment of the project's requirements is crucial. Choose wisely.

Remember, selecting a license isn't a trivial decision; it has lasting implications for your project and your relationship with the community surrounding it. The MIT License, despite its simplicity, demands an understanding of its freedoms and limitations to make it a genuinely effective choice. Weighing the advantages of flexibility against potential risks ensures the most informed and responsible application of this widely-used license. Don't just accept it because it's popular; instead, critically assess its fit with your project's specific context and long-term goals. The clarity and simplicity of the license shouldn't overshadow the critical thinking required for proper application.

2.3 Apache License 2.0

The Apache License 2.0, a popular choice for many open-source projects, offers a balance between permissive use and protecting the

original creators' rights. Its permissive nature allows for broad adoption and modification, fostering a collaborative environment. However, it also incorporates safeguards ensuring proper attribution and limiting liability for the licensor. Unlike more restrictive licenses, it doesn't require derivative works to also be open-sourced, offering more flexibility for commercial applications. This makes it attractive to businesses seeking to integrate open-source components into their proprietary software without facing the constraints of copyleft licenses.
Understanding the core tenets of the Apache License 2.0 is crucial. It grants users the right to use, modify, and distribute the software, including for commercial purposes. This freedom is a significant driver of its widespread adoption. The license, however, demands that all copies and substantial portions of the software include the original copyright notice and the license itself. This simple requirement ensures proper attribution to the original creators, a fundamental aspect of open-source ethics. Furthermore, the license disclaims any warranty, explicitly stating that the software is provided "as is," without any guarantee of its functionality or fitness for a particular purpose. This aspect shifts the responsibility for ensuring the software's suitability onto the user, protecting the original developers from potential legal liabilities.
One of the key distinctions of the Apache License 2.0 lies in its handling of patents. It includes a patent grant, a crucial element protecting users against potential patent infringement claims from the licensor. This means that if the licensor holds any patents relevant to the software, they are implicitly granted to users for the use and distribution of the software under the license. This is a powerful safeguard, offering users greater confidence and reducing legal risks associated with adopting and deploying the software. Conversely, it does not require users to grant their patents back to the licensor, thereby preserving their own intellectual property rights. This dual approach—protecting both the user and the licensor—is a defining characteristic of the Apache License's balanced approach. It's a key reason for its appeal across diverse software development landscapes.
The license's relatively simple language contributes to its widespread use. It is designed for clarity and ease of understanding, even for those

without extensive legal expertise. This user-friendliness is a significant advantage, as it reduces the complexities often associated with software licensing. The clear and concise wording minimizes the need for extensive legal interpretation, simplifying the process of integration and adoption for both individuals and organizations. This contrasts with some licenses that are significantly more complex and often necessitate legal consultation before use, increasing cost and potentially delaying projects. The Apache License 2.0's focus on readability reduces this barrier to entry.

However, while simplicity is beneficial, users must still exercise caution and ensure full comprehension. While the license is straightforward, certain nuances require careful consideration, particularly regarding the extent of allowed modifications and the implications of attribution requirements. Simply including the copyright notice isn't enough; it's crucial to understand what constitutes a "substantial portion" of the software to maintain compliance. Ignoring these details can lead to unintended legal consequences, potentially undermining the benefits of using the license. For larger projects or commercially significant applications, consultation with legal counsel specializing in open-source licenses remains advisable to prevent future complications.

In conclusion, the Apache License 2.0 is a well-structured, widely-used open-source license offering a flexible and practical balance between permissive use and legal protection. Its clear language, patent grant, and disclaimer of warranty make it an attractive choice for numerous projects, encouraging collaboration and innovation. However, users should not underestimate the importance of careful review and, if necessary, professional legal advice to ensure compliance with its terms, maximizing the benefits while minimizing potential risks associated with its implementation. The widespread adoption of this license showcases its efficacy as a robust framework for open-source collaboration. Its enduring popularity speaks volumes to its suitability for both small individual projects and large-scale commercial endeavors. Understanding its nuances is vital for anyone working within the open-source ecosystem.

2.4 BSD Licenses

The Berkeley Software Distribution (BSD) licenses represent a family of permissive open-source licenses, known for their flexibility and minimal restrictions. Unlike copyleft licenses like the GPL, BSD licenses prioritize freedom of use and modification, allowing developers significant leeway in incorporating the licensed software into their projects, even commercial ones, without needing to open-source their derivative work. This permissive nature has made BSD licenses incredibly popular, particularly for libraries and components used in larger software projects. Their simplicity and clear terms contribute to their widespread adoption.

Several variations of the BSD license exist, each with slight nuances, but they all share a core set of permissions. The original BSD license, appearing in the early days of the Berkeley Unix operating system, is quite concise. Later versions, such as the "Revised BSD License" (often called the "3-Clause BSD License") and the "Simplified BSD License" (or "2-Clause BSD License"), refined and streamlined the original, removing some clauses. Understanding these differences is crucial, as subtle variations in the wording can impact the rights granted and obligations imposed.

The core permission granted by all BSD licenses involves the right to use, modify, and distribute the software, including modified versions, for any purpose, including commercial applications. This freedom extends to both the source code and the compiled versions. The most significant difference between the 2-clause and 3-clause versions lies in the presence of an advertising clause. The 3-Clause BSD License includes a clause stating that any advertising materials mentioning the software must acknowledge its origin and the fact it is licensed under the BSD license. This clause is absent from the 2-Clause BSD License, offering even greater flexibility.

Choosing between the 2-clause and 3-clause versions largely depends on individual project preferences. Some developers might favor the slightly more restrictive 3-clause license for ethical considerations, to ensure proper attribution. Others prefer the complete freedom and lack of obligation offered by the 2-clause version. However, this decision typically carries no significant impact in practical terms. The licensing differences are minor, and the core permissions remain remarkably similar across all BSD variants.

Despite their permissive nature, it is essential to note that BSD licenses don't relinquish all rights. The copyright remains with the original authors, and the license serves as a permission grant, not a waiver of copyright. Therefore, modifications and redistribution must always comply with the license's terms. Attribution, although not strictly required in the 2-clause version, is a generally accepted and ethically sound practice. Crediting original authors promotes transparency and builds a positive community ethos.

A thorough understanding of the nuances of the BSD licenses is important, particularly regarding potential copyright issues. While the licenses offer considerable freedom, they do not negate the fundamental principles of copyright law. The license only grants specific rights to users and developers; it doesn't override the underlying copyright held by the original author or authors. This means that while you can freely use, modify, and distribute the software, you are still not permitted to claim ownership of the original code.

Moreover, the BSD licenses, like all open-source licenses, don't offer any warranty or guarantee of functionality. The software is provided "as is," without any express or implied warranties of merchantability or fitness for a specific purpose. Users and developers assume all risks associated with the use of the software. This "as is" provision is common in open-source licensing and underscores the need for thorough testing and evaluation before incorporating the software into any project. This lack of warranty does not imply negligence or disregard for quality; it simply reflects the nature of open-source development and the limitations of the license itself. It places the onus of responsibility squarely on the user.

The permissive nature of BSD licenses is a double-edged sword. While incredibly flexible, it might not provide the same level of control or community governance seen in copyleft licenses. Projects using BSD licenses might find themselves without the same strong community

support or strict adherence to certain development standards found in licenses requiring the release of derivative works under similar terms. This trade-off between flexibility and community control is a key factor to consider when selecting a license for your own project. The choice depends on the project's goals and the desired level of collaboration.
In conclusion, BSD licenses offer a powerful tool for developers seeking a permissive approach to software licensing. Their simplicity, minimal restrictions, and wide acceptance have led to their widespread adoption. However, it's crucial to carefully consider the specific requirements and implications of each BSD variant and to understand the ongoing responsibilities associated with utilizing licensed software, even within the permissive confines of a BSD license. Understanding the nuances of these licenses ensures compliance and fosters ethical practices in the open-source community. This careful consideration and responsible use underpin the success of open-source projects and their continuous evolution.

2.5 MPL and LGPL

The Mozilla Public License (MPL) and the Lesser General Public License (LGPL) represent distinct approaches within the open-source licensing landscape. Unlike the GPL's strict copyleft, which requires derivative works to also be open-sourced, the MPL offers a more flexible approach. It's designed to encourage collaboration while allowing for some proprietary elements within projects that incorporate MPL-licensed code. This makes it particularly attractive for projects where a mixture of open and closed-source components is desirable. The choice between the two ultimately depends on the project's specific goals and the developer's desired level of control over how their work is used and distributed.
The MPL, for instance, features a key distinction: it only mandates the licensing of modified portions of the original work. If you use the original code without modification, you are not obligated to release your modifications under the MPL, a stark contrast to the GPL. This dual li-

censing mechanism provides a bridge between open and closed-source worlds, facilitating contributions while granting significant freedoms to derivative developers. Understanding the specific requirements of this license is essential, emphasizing its unique characteristics in terms of copyleft implications.

Consider a scenario where a developer integrates an MPL-licensed library into their proprietary software. Under the MPL, the developer is not obligated to open-source their entire project; only the modifications made to the library itself need to follow the MPL's terms. This flexibility empowers businesses to leverage open-source components without relinquishing complete control over their product. It allows for a more balanced approach, considering both the advantages of collaboration and the protective measures necessary for proprietary software. The emphasis here is on selective openness, granting freedom to modify and distribute but not requiring reciprocal open-sourcing of the entire project.

The LGPL, on the other hand, adopts a slightly different strategy while maintaining a core commitment to open-source principles. It's often described as a "weak copyleft" license, allowing for linking against LGPL-licensed libraries without requiring the entire application to be released under the same license. This makes the LGPL exceptionally suitable for creating libraries or components intended for use within larger projects. It strikes a compromise between open-source values and the needs of developers working with proprietary software. This flexible approach encourages wider adoption of open-source libraries within commercial applications.

This characteristic distinguishes the LGPL from the GPL, which mandates that modifications to the code must be made available under the GPL license. This is precisely the area where the flexibility of the LGPL shines. A developer using an LGPL-licensed library can incorporate it into a proprietary system without necessarily exposing their own modifications. It represents a vital option when integrating open-source tools into a commercial product requires a degree of proprietary code protection. This consideration is paramount when strategizing how to leverage open-source libraries without compromising the over-

all commercial value of the application.
The practical implications are significant. Imagine a game developer utilizing an LGPL-licensed physics engine. The developer can freely incorporate this engine, enhancing their game's capabilities without needing to make their game's source code public. However, should they modify the physics engine itself, those modifications must be released under the LGPL. This selective copyleft approach avoids the complexities of the GPL's stricter requirements, granting a greater degree of freedom within the context of commercial software development. It elegantly balances the interests of both open-source contribution and commercial application.
Therefore, the choice between the MPL and LGPL necessitates a careful consideration of project goals, intended distribution methods, and the desired level of openness. It is not merely a matter of selecting a license; it is a fundamental decision influencing the project's development trajectory and how it interacts with the broader software ecosystem. It is critical to understand the nuances of each, aligning them with the project's specific requirements and objectives. Choosing the wrong license could have unexpected and, potentially, negative legal and commercial consequences.
Moreover, understanding the legal ramifications is paramount. While both licenses promote open-source ideals, their respective legal implications differ considerably. The MPL's more permissive approach enables a greater degree of freedom, potentially easing commercial integration. Conversely, the LGPL's restrictions regarding modified components must be diligently addressed. This is crucial for compliance and avoiding potential legal entanglements. Failure to comply with the respective terms and conditions could result in legal action, potentially harming the reputation and profitability of a project or business.
In conclusion, while both the MPL and LGPL serve as powerful tools in the open-source arsenal, their fundamental differences necessitate careful evaluation before implementation. Their distinct licensing approaches cater to different project needs and commercial goals. A thorough understanding of each license's stipulations is crucial for ensuring legal compliance and fostering successful integration within both

open and closed-source projects. The choice must be deliberate and strategic, reflecting the unique characteristics and requirements of the specific software development endeavor. It is a choice that should not be taken lightly.

3 License Selection & Compliance

Understanding your project's needs is paramount. Do you intend for your software to be freely modifiable and redistributable by others, or do you prefer to maintain more control over its evolution and commercial use? Consider the level of collaboration you desire; an open and permissive license fosters broader community involvement, while a restrictive license might better suit projects with specific commercial goals. Each choice has implications, and careful consideration is vital. Choosing wrongly can lead to legal headaches and lost opportunities.
The MIT License, for example, offers a highly permissive approach. It grants users extensive freedom to use, modify, and distribute the software, even commercially, with minimal obligations. This makes it appealing for projects aiming for widespread adoption and rapid iteration. However, this permissiveness comes with a trade-off; it offers less protection for your intellectual property compared to a copyleft license.
Conversely, the GNU General Public License (GPL) is a copyleft license. This means any derivative works must also be licensed under the GPL, ensuring that modifications remain open-source. This fosters a collaborative environment and prevents proprietary "forking," but it might deter commercial entities seeking to incorporate your software into closed-source products. The GPL's various versions add layers of complexity, making understanding their nuances crucial for correct implementation. GPLv3, for instance, has specific clauses address-

ing software-as-a-service and digital rights management that weren't present in earlier versions.

Legal compliance isn't just about understanding the license text; it's about actively adhering to its terms. Proper attribution, clearly displaying the license terms, and avoiding actions that violate the license's stipulations are essential. Ignoring these aspects can lead to legal disputes, which can be expensive and damaging to your project's reputation. Negligence is not a defense in legal matters, so understanding and implementing the terms from the beginning is essential for long-term success and avoidance of costly errors.

Consider the implications of your chosen license on potential future collaborations. If you plan to integrate your project with other open-source software, compatibility is key. Choosing a license that conflicts with existing licenses can create friction and hinder collaboration. A thorough understanding of license compatibility is paramount, as it can prevent potential legal clashes down the line, saving your company both money and reputation. Consult with legal professionals to ensure that all necessary agreements are in place before proceeding.

Attribution is not merely a formality; it's a legal obligation under many licenses. Properly crediting original authors and licensors isn't just ethically sound; it's crucial for avoiding copyright infringement claims. Failing to provide accurate and visible attribution can lead to legal action. It's better to err on the side of over-attribution than under-attribution, as this ensures compliance and avoids legal complications. Remember that simple acknowledgment is often not sufficient; the precise method of attribution is generally specified within the license itself.

Patent issues are a significant consideration, particularly if your software incorporates patented technologies. Open-source licenses typically don't grant immunity from patent infringement. Understanding the potential patent landscape associated with your project and obtaining necessary licenses or waivers is crucial to avoid costly litigation. A patent attorney can provide guidance and help mitigate this risk. It's advisable to conduct thorough patent searches before committing to a license to ensure you won't run into conflicts later.

Liability considerations extend beyond copyright and patent issues. Depending on the license, you might assume certain liabilities regarding the software's functionality and potential damages. Understanding these liabilities and implementing appropriate disclaimers and limitations of liability is vital to protect your interests. Consult legal counsel to tailor disclaimers and limitations to your project's specific needs, as they vary greatly depending on jurisdiction and context. This will help you to avoid unforeseen legal issues later on.

The best approach is proactive compliance. Engage legal counsel early in the process to select the appropriate license and understand the implications for your project. This is crucial; obtaining legal advice early minimizes risks and prevents potential disputes from arising. Proactive compliance is not just a matter of avoiding legal battles; it's also about fostering a trusting relationship with the community and promoting the long-term success of the project.

Ultimately, license selection and compliance are integral to the success and sustainability of any open-source project. Careful consideration, legal guidance, and proactive adherence to license terms are essential for fostering collaboration, protecting your interests, and contributing to the vibrant ecosystem of open-source software. A thorough understanding is not merely recommended; it's crucial for long-term project health and legal security. Failure to comply can result in severe legal consequences, hindering the potential of the project entirely. Therefore, prioritize this crucial aspect.

3.1 Choosing the Right License

Choosing the right open-source license is crucial, impacting everything from your project's usage to its potential for commercialization. Get this wrong, and you could face legal challenges, stifle collaboration, or limit your project's reach. A well-chosen license, conversely, can attract contributors, boost adoption, and even become a key component of your business strategy.

The selection process isn't about picking the most popular license; it's about finding the best fit for your specific goals and circumstances. Consider your project's intended use: will it be a personal tool, a library for others to incorporate into their software, or the foundation of a commercial product? The answer dictates the level of permissiveness needed. Think carefully; the consequences of a poor decision can be significant. A poorly chosen license could severely limit your ability to profit from the hard work of development.

Permissive licenses, like the MIT and BSD licenses, offer maximum freedom to users. They require minimal attribution and place few restrictions on modification or commercial use. These are ideal for projects aiming for broad adoption, encouraging contributions without demanding reciprocal sharing of improvements. However, this freedom comes with a trade-off: you have less control over how your software is used or modified. The lack of restrictions might also make it difficult to enforce branding or track derivative works. It's essential to evaluate what level of control you wish to maintain.

Conversely, copyleft licenses, such as the GPL, demand that any derivative works also remain open-source under the same license. This encourages a collaborative ecosystem, fostering a strong community around your project. It can be extremely beneficial for collaborative efforts, as everyone shares improvements. However, this strong-arming of subsequent projects into open-source can be a substantial barrier to commercialization or integration within proprietary systems. It's important to understand which types of projects benefit from this sort of licensing.

Beyond the core distinctions between permissive and copyleft, consider nuances within each license family. For example, the GPL has several versions, each with subtle but important differences in requirements. Similarly, the BSD licenses have different clauses and stipulations, ranging from more permissive to somewhat more restrictive. Diligent research is essential before settling on a specific license. Don't just skim the summary; read the entire text of the license itself.

Don't underestimate the legal complexities involved. While many open-source licenses seem straightforward, their interpretation can become tricky in real-world scenarios. Consulting a lawyer specializ-

ing in intellectual property law is highly recommended, particularly for complex projects or those with commercial implications. This proactive approach can save you headaches and potential legal battles down the line. It is a small investment with potentially significant returns.
Remember, your chosen license isn't just a legal document; it's a statement about your project's philosophy and intended use. A well-considered choice sets the stage for future growth, attracting contributors and users while protecting your intellectual property rights. Understanding the implications of various licenses is vital to your project's success, and to your own future. So take the time; make the right choice. The repercussions of choosing poorly can be difficult to recover from.

3.2 Legal Compliance

Understanding and adhering to the legal stipulations of open-source licenses is paramount. Ignoring these requirements can lead to costly lawsuits and reputational damage, undermining the very collaborative spirit open source fosters. This chapter focuses on practical strategies for ensuring legal compliance, transforming potential pitfalls into opportunities for robust project development.
Begin by meticulously reviewing the chosen license's terms. Don't just skim; understand every clause, every caveat. Consider using a legally-trained professional if the license is complex, particularly if your project involves commercial applications or integrates with other software. Remember, a simple misunderstanding can have significant legal ramifications. Professional legal advice, while costly upfront, can prevent far greater expenses later. The cost-benefit analysis often favors proactive legal consultation.
Attribution is a cornerstone of many open-source licenses. This isn't just about giving credit; it's a legal obligation. Failure to properly attribute original authors can constitute copyright infringement, triggering legal action. Maintain detailed records of all sources, including licenses, versions, and author names. Such meticulous record-keeping

serves as irrefutable proof of compliance, protecting you from potential accusations of infringement. This is crucial, not just for legal reasons, but also for establishing credibility and transparency within the open-source community.

Patent issues present a unique challenge in the open-source world. While open-source licenses generally don't grant patent rights, the use of open-source software might inadvertently infringe on existing patents. Conduct thorough patent searches before integrating any third-party components. This proactive approach reduces your liability significantly. Consult a patent attorney if uncertainties arise; their expertise is indispensable in navigating the complexities of intellectual property rights within the open-source ecosystem. Understanding the intricacies of patent law is critical, as even unintentional infringement can lead to legal trouble. A proactive strategy is far better than reactive litigation.

Liability is another crucial area. Open-source licenses typically limit the liability of the original authors. However, if you modify or redistribute the software, your liability might increase. Clearly state the extent of your modifications and provide appropriate disclaimers. Furthermore, implement rigorous testing procedures to minimize the risk of bugs and security vulnerabilities. This meticulous approach demonstrates responsibility and minimizes potential legal risks associated with software malfunctions or security breaches.

Staying informed about license updates is essential. Licenses are not static; they can be updated to reflect evolving legal norms and community expectations. Regularly review the licenses of all software components used in your project. By staying updated, you maintain compliance and ensure your project remains legally sound. Regular updates are essential for maintaining not only legal compliance but also for leveraging the latest improvements and security patches in the open-source software you utilize. Keeping up with changes ensures that your project continues to benefit from the advancements in the technologies upon which it's built.

Community engagement doesn't just enhance collaboration; it also indirectly helps with legal compliance. Active participation in open-source communities provides access to valuable insights and expertise from other developers and legal professionals. This fosters a shared understanding of licensing best practices and helps to avoid common pitfalls. By actively engaging in the community, you become part of a network that offers support, advice, and resources that can help you proactively manage and address legal compliance issues. It enhances your understanding and prevents many problems before they even arise. Finally, remember that legal compliance isn't merely a box to be ticked; it's an ongoing process. It requires vigilance, attention to detail, and a proactive approach to managing risk. Regularly review your practices, stay informed about evolving legal frameworks and community standards, and don't hesitate to seek professional advice when needed. This commitment to ongoing legal compliance fosters trust within the community, protects your project, and allows you to fully reap the rewards of open-source collaboration.

4 Practical Aspects of Licensing

Understanding copyright is fundamental. It's the automatic legal protection granted to creators of original works, including software code. Open-source licenses don't negate copyright; they grant specific permissions to use, modify, and distribute the software under defined conditions. Attribution, often a key requirement, means properly crediting the original authors – it's not just a nice gesture; it's a legal obligation under many licenses. Failure to provide proper attribution can lead to legal complications, ranging from cease-and-desist letters to more serious litigation. Therefore, meticulous attention to the license's attribution requirements is paramount. Understanding the nuances of copyright within the context of open-source licenses is crucial for avoiding legal pitfalls. This necessitates careful reading of the license text itself, as well as seeking legal counsel if ambiguity arises. Remember, navigating these complexities successfully safeguards both the creator and the user.

Patent issues introduce another layer of complexity. Software often incorporates patented technologies, either knowingly or unknowingly. Using open-source software doesn't automatically grant immunity from patent infringement. If your project uses a component covered by a patent, you could face legal action from the patent holder, regardless of the software's license. Therefore, diligent due diligence is essential. This involves researching whether the open-source components you use are free from patent encumbrances. While complete certainty is impossible, taking proactive steps to mitigate risk—such as choosing licenses with explicit patent grants or incorporating only well-vetted components—can significantly reduce exposure. The open-source community itself is not necessarily a shield against patent claims.

Liability is a significant consideration, particularly for those distributing or modifying open-source software. The license usually doesn't absolve you of responsibility for defects or harm caused by the software. If your modifications introduce bugs that cause damage, you could be held liable. This underscores the critical importance of thorough testing and documentation before releasing any modifications. Furthermore, even if you haven't altered the original code, you might still be held liable depending on your role in distributing or promoting the software. This liability extends to both direct and indirect damages caused by any defects. It's important to remember that simply using open-source code doesn't automatically absolve you of responsibility for problems. Consequently, thorough testing and due diligence are vital to mitigate risk, and professional legal advice is recommended. The responsibility rests on understanding that incorporating open-source software into a larger project doesn't necessarily diminish liability.

Many believe choosing a license is a simple matter, but it's a crucial decision with long-term consequences. Selecting the appropriate license depends on your project's goals and how you want others to use your work. Permissive licenses, such as MIT or BSD, grant considerable freedom to users, while copyleft licenses, like GPL, require that modifications be shared under the same license. The choice between these extremes often hinges on balancing the benefits of community collaboration against the desire to maintain control over your creation. The impact of the license selection transcends the initial release; it affects future development, collaboration opportunities, and potential commercial applications. It's not merely a technical detail; it shapes the entire lifecycle of your software. A hasty decision may lead to unforeseen complications later, emphasizing the need for careful consideration. This is not just about compliance, but about strategically shaping your

project's future.
Understanding these practical aspects is critical for successful navigation of the open-source landscape. It's not enough to simply choose a license; you must fully grasp its implications concerning copyright, patents, and liability. Proactive risk mitigation through thorough due diligence, careful testing, and informed decision-making is essential for avoiding potential legal issues. Remember that while open-source offers many advantages, it also introduces unique legal complexities that require careful attention. Open source isn't a legal loophole but a framework with its own set of rules and responsibilities. The journey involves proactive engagement, not passive compliance. By meticulously addressing these practical facets, you can confidently leverage the power of open-source while safeguarding yourself and your contributions. Engaging with the legal intricacies is not an option; it's an obligation, and it sets the foundation for responsible participation within this vibrant ecosystem. Approaching licensing with a holistic understanding offers not only legal protection but also fosters sustainable and collaborative open-source practices.

4.1 Copyright and Attribution

Understanding copyright is fundamental when working with open-source software. It's the legal right granted to the creator of an original work, including software code. This right protects their expression, not the underlying idea. Therefore, you can't copyright the concept of a spreadsheet program, but you can copyright your specific implementation of one. Failure to respect these rights can lead to legal repercussions, ranging from cease-and-desist letters to costly lawsuits. Navigating this landscape requires careful attention to detail and a thorough understanding of the chosen license. Ignoring copyright can severely damage your reputation and possibly your career. The consequences can be far-reaching and can severely impact the financial and legal standing of any project. Transparency and respect for intellectual property rights are paramount in open-source communities. Understanding the intricacies of copyright protection is not just legally prudent; it's a moral imperative that builds trust within these collaborative environments.

Attribution, closely tied to copyright, specifies how to give credit to the original creators of the software or components you use. Open-source licenses often mandate specific attribution requirements, usually including the name of the copyright holder, the license name, and a link to the license text. This isn't just a formality; it's a legal obligation. Neglecting to properly attribute can lead to license violations and potential legal battles. Always meticulously document the origin of every piece of code, library, or resource incorporated into your project. This detailed record not only ensures compliance but also aids in the future tracking of updates and potential issues, demonstrating clear and precise provenance of your materials. A well-maintained attribution record offers considerable advantages in terms of intellectual honesty and proactive legal compliance.

Different licenses have varying attribution requirements. Some licenses may demand simple copyright notices within the source code, while others might require specific statements in documentation or even on the software's website or packaging. Always refer to the specific license text for definitive guidance—don't rely on assumptions or generalized information. Each license differs in its requirements, and only a careful reading will allow for safe and respectful usage. Don't treat it as a chore, it is the only way to use the work and not find yourself in a difficult legal situation. Pay close attention to every term and condition. Misinterpreting a license's terms can lead to unintended consequences, potentially jeopardizing the legitimacy of your work and leading to considerable legal issues.

Consider the case of a developer incorporating a third-party library into their open-source project. If the library is licensed under the GPL, the developer must ensure the entire project is also released under the GPL, respecting its "viral" nature. This includes providing proper attribution to the original library authors. This is a very important element, not only for legal purposes but also for collaboration, giving credit to developers which helped your project. Neglecting this aspect can result in legal challenges from the original library's copyright holders. This example clearly demonstrates the interdependency between copyright and attribution in open source development. You are not only required to comply with copyright and attribution regulations, but are also encouraged to foster respectful collaboration and communication with the developers whose code you use in your project.

Beyond the legal aspects, proper attribution is a matter of professional ethics and community respect. Giving credit where it's due builds trust and fosters collaboration. It acknowledges the contributions of others and promotes a sense of shared ownership within the open-source community. Attributing properly helps to build a more healthy and respectful collaborative environment, helping everyone. It allows for easier tracking of sources and facilitates community participation. This is not a simple matter of legality, it is an essential part of the collaborative ethos of open-source development. Building and maintaining respectful relationships within the open-source community is crucial for long-term success and growth.

Finally, when in doubt, seek legal counsel. Copyright law can be complex, and consulting a lawyer specialized in intellectual property can prevent future legal complications. The cost of prevention can be extremely cheap compared to the legal battles which might happen if you're not attentive to detail. Don't hesitate to ask for professional help. It's a prudent investment that protects your project, your reputation, and your resources from potential problems that can arise from legal and procedural errors. Investing in professional advice is often a cost-effective measure that reduces future risks and potential costs. This proactive approach promotes a more secure and well-managed open-source project and contributes to your overall success. This precaution can save you much time and considerable money.

4.2 Patent Issues

Patents represent a significant hurdle in the open-source landscape, often clashing with the collaborative and freely-shared nature of the movement. Understanding patent issues is crucial for anyone involved in open-source software, from developers and users to organizations and businesses. Unlike copyrights which protect the expression of an idea, patents protect inventions themselves—a specific process, machine, manufacture, composition of matter, or improvement thereof. This difference leads to unique challenges within the open-source ecosystem.

A major concern stems from the fact that an open-source project might unknowingly incorporate patented technology. This could happen through the use of third-party libraries, components, or even algorithms integrated into the software. A company subsequently commercializing a derivative of that open-source project might find itself facing patent infringement lawsuits, a potentially expensive and time-consuming ordeal. Such lawsuits can lead to significant financial burdens, including licensing fees, legal costs, and even potential injunctions that could halt product development and sales.

The open-source community typically addresses this through various strategies, none of which offer a foolproof solution. One common approach is the use of open-source licenses that include patent grants. For instance, some licenses explicitly state that the licensor grants a non-exclusive, worldwide, royalty-free patent license to use the covered software, mitigating the risk to users. However, it's important to realize that such a license only covers patents held by the licensor; it doesn't protect against infringement of patents held by third parties. Carefully reviewing the license terms is essential to understanding the extent of the patent protection offered.

Another strategy involves thorough due diligence before integrating any third-party components into an open-source project. This might include searching patent databases for relevant patents and reviewing the licensing terms of any external libraries. While this approach is proactive, it's labor-intensive and can't guarantee complete protection. Identifying all potential patent infringements is nearly impossible, given the sheer volume and sometimes ambiguous nature of patent applications.

Furthermore, there's the challenge of patent trolls, entities that acquire patents primarily to assert them against others and extract licensing fees, rather than to develop and commercialize the related inventions. These entities often target open-source projects, recognizing that the decentralized nature of the community can make it difficult to mount a comprehensive defense.

Navigating the complexities of patents requires a multi-pronged approach. While open-source licenses and due diligence are important first steps, they don't eliminate all risk. A strong community and active communication are essential. This involves maintaining open and transparent communication among developers, users, and contributors. A vibrant community can more effectively identify potential patent issues, react promptly, and coordinate defense strategies.

Beyond community efforts, considering the legal framework is equally crucial. Understanding the relevant patent laws in the jurisdictions where the software is used or commercialized is paramount. Seeking expert legal counsel is highly recommended, especially when commercializing an open-source project or facing a potential patent infringement claim. Legal expertise can help in navigating complex patent litigation, assessing the potential risks, and developing effective strategies for mitigation.

In conclusion, patents pose a significant challenge to the open-source world. While the collaborative nature of open source fosters innovation, it can also inadvertently lead to patent infringement. The combination of careful license selection, proactive due diligence, robust community engagement, and legal expertise offers the best approach for mitigating these risks. Understanding the limitations of each strategy and implementing a multifaceted approach is key to successfully navigating the patent landscape within the open-source environment. Remember, proactive planning and a well-informed approach are essential for protecting both the project and its contributors.

4.3 Liability Considerations

Understanding the potential liabilities associated with open-source software is crucial for both developers and users. While the collaborative nature of open source fosters innovation, it also introduces complexities regarding responsibility and accountability. Negligence in adhering to license terms, for example, can lead to legal repercussions, including costly lawsuits and reputational damage. Therefore, a proactive approach to understanding liability is essential.

This isn't merely about avoiding legal trouble; it's about building a sustainable and trustworthy ecosystem. Clear understanding of your obligations under a chosen license protects you from unforeseen issues. It allows for collaborative development without the constant fear of infringement. Think of it as a foundation upon which a strong, collaborative open-source project is built. Ignoring this aspect risks compromising the entire structure.

One significant area of liability stems from the use of components within a larger project. If a library or module incorporated into your software contains a bug leading to damage or financial loss, determining who is responsible—the original developer, the maintainer, or you—can become a complex legal battle. Thorough vetting of third-party components and understanding their respective licenses is paramount. Due diligence in this area is not simply good practice; it's a necessary safeguard.

The type of license plays a pivotal role. Permissive licenses, such as the MIT License, often place less onus on downstream users, granting broad rights. However, even these licenses stipulate conditions, often concerning attribution and patent claims. Conversely, copyleft licenses like the GPL impose stricter obligations, requiring any derivative work to also be open-sourced under the same terms. Understanding these variations is crucial for risk mitigation. Failing to comply with these conditions can lead to severe consequences.

Copyright infringement is another key concern. Improper use of copyrighted material, even unintentionally, can result in legal action. This highlights the need for careful review of all incorporated materials and clear documentation of their source and license. A robust system of tracking and documenting the provenance of all components is a simple, yet effective, method of minimizing risk. This also promotes transparency and facilitates easy investigation in case of disputes.

Patent infringement presents a more subtle yet potentially severe liability. Open-source projects might inadvertently use patented technology, exposing contributors and users to legal challenges. While open-source licenses don't inherently protect against patent claims, understanding the patent landscape surrounding your project and actively seeking out information on potential conflicts is a crucial preventative measure. Ignoring this aspect can lead to financial ruin and protracted legal battles.
Moreover, consider the liability implications of your project's intended use. If your open-source software is used in a critical system, such as medical equipment or financial transactions, the potential for significant damage from errors is greatly magnified. This necessitates increased rigor in testing and quality assurance. Understanding the potential impact and conducting rigorous testing helps mitigate potential liabilities related to errors or malfunctions.
Furthermore, the responsibility for security vulnerabilities deserves special attention. While open-source projects often benefit from community scrutiny and rapid bug fixing, security breaches can still occur and lead to significant consequences for users. Proactive security practices, timely patching, and transparent communication are crucial in building user trust and reducing legal vulnerabilities. Neglecting security can lead to far-reaching damage, beyond simple financial loss.
Ultimately, proactive management of open-source software liability involves a multi-faceted approach. It's not just about understanding the legal ramifications of various licenses; it's about establishing a culture of responsible development, fostering transparency within the project, and proactively addressing potential vulnerabilities. This includes thorough component vetting, rigorous testing, clear licensing, and constant attention to the evolving legal landscape. It's an ongoing process that ensures the long-term success and sustainability of the project.
The process of mitigating risk begins with clear communication. This includes clearly stating the license terms, making attribution information readily available, and documenting the provenance of all included components. This clarity minimizes confusion and potential misunderstandings which can lead to legal conflicts. It's a straightforward, yet remarkably effective safeguard.

Beyond clear communication, regularly reviewing and updating licenses and associated documentation is a crucial preventative measure. Changes in project scope, addition of new components, and updates to underlying libraries can significantly impact liability. Proactive adaptation to these changes helps prevent future disputes. It's a long-term investment in the project's viability.

Remember, minimizing liability isn't simply about avoiding lawsuits; it's about fostering trust and collaboration within the open-source community. By diligently understanding and managing the complexities of open-source licenses, developers can build strong, sustainable, and responsible projects that contribute positively to the broader ecosystem. This is not just a legal necessity, it is a crucial part of participating in the collaborative spirit of open source.

5 Open Source Communities

Participating in open-source communities offers invaluable learning experiences and networking opportunities. You'll gain practical skills by working alongside experienced developers, contributing to real-world projects, and tackling challenging problems. This collaborative environment fosters rapid skill development and exposes you to diverse coding styles and best practices, ultimately accelerating your professional growth. The collaborative nature provides a unique environment for learning and growth beyond what typical academic or professional settings could provide. Your contributions, no matter how small, can make a tangible difference, boosting your confidence and showcasing your abilities to potential employers.

Finding a project that aligns with your interests and skill level is crucial for a positive experience. Begin by exploring popular platforms like GitHub and GitLab, searching for projects with active communities and well-defined contribution guidelines. Don't jump into the largest projects immediately; start with smaller, more manageable projects. This allows you to learn the ropes without feeling overwhelmed. Look for projects actively seeking contributions, often indicated by "Good First Issue" labels or similar markings, and carefully read the project's documentation, including contributing guidelines, before jumping in. Familiarize yourself with the project's codebase and understand its current challenges and planned features.

Effective communication is paramount within open-source communities. Engaging respectfully and professionally is essential. Clearly articulate your ideas, ask clarifying questions when needed, and actively participate in discussions. Before submitting code, ensure it adheres to the project's style guidelines and coding standards. Thoroughly test your contributions before submitting them to avoid introducing bugs or breaking existing functionality. Regularly check for updates and feedback, and be responsive to comments and suggestions from other contributors. Remember, collaboration is key; always maintain a professional demeanor, even when facing disagreements. Proactive communication builds strong relationships with other contributors.

Different open-source projects employ diverse governance models. Some utilize a benevolent dictator model, where a single individual holds ultimate authority. Others operate on a more democratic structure, with decision-making distributed among a council or committee. Understanding the governance model of a project is crucial for navigating its decision-making processes and contributing effectively. It's also important to familiarize yourself with the project's communication channels—mailing lists, forums, or chat platforms—and participate in ongoing discussions. Understanding how a project handles conflict resolution and decision-making will help you navigate its processes smoothly. This insight will help you understand how to submit bug reports, propose new features, or participate in design discussions.

Contributing to open source goes beyond just writing code. Testing, documentation, and community engagement are equally vital. Thoroughly testing software detects issues before they reach users, ensuring quality and stability. Well-written documentation improves usability and allows others to easily understand and contribute to the project. Active community participation strengthens the project's foundation and fosters collaboration. Don't underestimate the value of clear, concise documentation; it's as crucial as the code itself. You could write tutorials, create example applications, or update the existing documentation to make it more user-friendly and complete. These actions demonstrate your commitment and improve the project's accessibility for others. Remember that even small contributions, like fixing typos or improving code formatting, contribute significantly to the overall project health and show your commitment.

Building a strong reputation within an open-source community requires consistent effort and engagement. Consistently contributing high-quality code, participating in discussions, and helping others establishes your credibility. Over time, you'll gain recognition for your expertise, potentially leading to leadership roles within the community. It is crucial to be patient and persistent. Building a reputation takes time and consistent effort. Focus on consistently producing high-quality work, and your reputation will naturally grow. Remember to always give credit where credit is due and acknowledge the work of others. This positive reinforcement helps maintain a collaborative and supportive environment.
Open-source communities offer more than just technical skills development. They provide valuable networking opportunities, connecting you with like-minded individuals from around the world. This expanded network can lead to collaborations, mentorship opportunities, and potential job prospects. Building relationships within these communities can significantly broaden your professional horizons. Active participation enhances your profile, showcasing your skills and commitment to open source. Many employers value experience within these collaborative environments. By engaging in these communities, you significantly improve your job prospects, demonstrating valuable skills and experience. Attending meetups, conferences, and online discussions can foster stronger professional relationships. Your connections may extend beyond just coding, leading to new opportunities.

5.1 Community Engagement

Effective community engagement is paramount for the success of any open-source project. It fosters collaboration, attracts contributors, and ensures the ongoing development and improvement of the software. Building a thriving community requires a multifaceted approach, encompassing proactive communication, inclusive practices, and a clear understanding of community dynamics. Ignoring these aspects can lead to stagnation, conflicts, and ultimately, the failure of the project.

Participating actively within the community is more than just downloading the software; it's about contributing back. This might involve reporting bugs, suggesting improvements, writing documentation, or even directly contributing code. Each contribution, regardless of size, strengthens the project and demonstrates a commitment to its future. Regularly engaging with the project's discussions, whether through forums, mailing lists, or issue trackers, allows you to stay informed, understand the project's direction, and connect with other developers. This constant feedback loop is crucial for maintaining a healthy, vibrant community.

Establishing clear communication channels is essential for effective community engagement. This includes providing readily accessible documentation, establishing active communication platforms like forums or chat channels, and actively responding to inquiries and feedback. Prompt responses to issues and concerns demonstrate a commitment to the users and contributors, fostering trust and encouraging continued participation. A well-structured wiki or documentation site is invaluable; it serves as a central repository for information, reducing the need for repeated explanations and ensuring consistent communication.

Open-source communities thrive on inclusivity and diversity. Creating a welcoming environment where everyone feels comfortable contributing, regardless of their background or skill level, is crucial for growth. Establishing clear guidelines for conduct and encouraging respectful interactions among members promotes a positive and productive atmosphere. This fostering of a safe and inclusive space means actively addressing any instances of harassment or discrimination, setting a precedent of intolerance for such behavior and protecting vulnerable members. This might involve implementing robust moderation procedures and clear codes of conduct.

Understanding different community governance models is critical for navigating the complexities of open-source projects. Some projects operate under a benevolent dictator model, with a single leader making major decisions. Others utilize more democratic structures, such as consensus-based decision-making or collaborative governance models. Regardless of the model employed, transparency in decision-making processes and open communication about project direction are paramount. This ensures that all participants understand the reasoning behind choices made, which ultimately builds trust and encourages continued involvement. A thorough understanding of these different models allows for a more informed contribution to the community, ensuring participation is both effective and harmonious.

Mentorship programs within open-source communities offer invaluable support for both new and experienced contributors. Experienced developers can guide newcomers, offering assistance and guidance, while simultaneously strengthening their own leadership skills. This reciprocal mentoring relationship not only improves the onboarding experience but also fosters a supportive environment within the community. Such structured programs also create a sustainable growth model for the community itself, resulting in increased project stability and resilience.

Finally, remember that community engagement is an ongoing process. It requires consistent effort, dedication, and a genuine commitment to the project's success. By actively participating, contributing constructively, and fostering a welcoming and inclusive environment, you not only strengthen the project itself, but you also contribute to the broader open-source ecosystem. This collective contribution is integral to the continued health and vibrancy of the open-source world. The commitment to building and maintaining robust communities is crucial, as these communities represent the very heart of the open-source ethos, driving innovation and collaboration on a global scale. This symbiotic relationship between community and project success is essential to remember throughout the entire development cycle.

5.2 Contributing to Projects

Finding a project that aligns with your skills and interests is the first step. Browse platforms like GitHub, GitLab, and SourceForge; search for repositories tagged with technologies you're familiar with. Look beyond the sheer size of a project; smaller projects often have friendlier onboarding processes and offer quicker paths to meaningful contributions. Don't be afraid to delve into the project's documentation, exploring the "Contributing" guidelines meticulously. This is your roadmap. Understanding the project's workflow is paramount. Many projects utilize issue trackers (like Jira or GitHub Issues) to manage bug reports and feature requests. Familiarize yourself with the issue's lifecycle: from reporting and triage to resolution and closure. Participate in discussions surrounding issues that pique your interest; this demonstrates engagement and helps you grasp the project's needs. Before diving into code, understanding the project's coding style and conventions, often documented in a CONTRIBUTING.md file, is crucial for a smooth integration.

Start small. Don't aim for a major feature rewrite immediately; focus on manageable tasks such as fixing typos in documentation, improving testing, or addressing minor bug fixes. These seemingly small contributions build your experience and familiarity with the project, demonstrating your commitment and paving the way for larger contributions in the future. Remember that consistent, incremental contributions are valued far more than sporadic, grandiose attempts.

Effective communication is key within open-source communities. Engage respectfully with other contributors, asking clarifying questions when needed. Be responsive to feedback and suggestions; accept constructive criticism as an opportunity for improvement. Avoid dominating conversations and always be mindful of the community's time and energy. This collaborative nature requires patience and respect.

Once you've chosen a task, create a "pull request" (PR). This is a formal proposal to merge your changes into the main project repository. Clearly describe the changes you've made and refer to the relevant issue in your PR description. A well-written PR significantly enhances the chances of your contribution being accepted. Ensure your code adheres to the project's coding standards and is well-documented. Consider addressing potential review comments promptly and thoroughly.

Testing your changes rigorously is essential. This validates your work and ensures that your contributions don't introduce unintended side effects. Many projects rely on automated testing; familiarize yourself with the existing test suite and write tests that cover the aspects of your code. Thorough testing displays a professional approach and demonstrates your dedication to the project's quality.

After your contribution is merged, celebrate your success! But remember this is just the beginning. Continue to engage with the community, monitoring issues, participating in discussions, and actively looking for opportunities to improve the project. Open source is a continuous journey of learning, collaboration, and growth. Each contribution strengthens your understanding of software development and your position within the wider open-source ecosystem.

Persistence is vital. Don't be discouraged by initial setbacks; rejection of a PR is often a learning opportunity. Carefully examine feedback, revise your work based on that feedback, and resubmit. Your determination to learn and improve will be recognized by the community. The path to contributing meaningfully to open source projects is not always linear, but the rewards—both personal and professional—are substantial and lasting. This iterative process of learning and contributing is what truly defines the experience. Remember that this is a long-term commitment that requires ongoing participation and patience, but that's part of its value. Open source is not a sprint; it's a marathon.

5.3 Governance Models

Effective governance is the backbone of any thriving open-source project. Without a clearly defined structure and decision-making process, projects can quickly become chaotic, leading to stagnation, internal conflict, and ultimately, failure. Choosing the right model requires careful consideration of the project's size, goals, and community dynamics. A well-structured governance model fosters collaboration, ensures transparency, and promotes sustainable growth. It's not a one-size-fits-all solution; the best approach is highly context-dependent.

Many projects, especially those starting small, operate under a benevolent dictator model. A single individual, often the initial creator, holds ultimate authority. This can be efficient in the early stages, allowing for rapid decision-making and a clear direction. However, as the project grows, this centralized control can become a bottleneck, hindering participation and innovation. Scalability becomes a major challenge, and the project's future might hinge on the single individual's continued involvement and capacity. This inherent risk is something to carefully assess.

A more distributed approach involves a leadership council or steering committee. Members are usually elected by the community, representing different areas of expertise or user interests. This model fosters a sense of shared ownership and responsibility, promoting inclusivity and preventing a single point of failure. Decisions are made collaboratively, requiring consensus or a weighted voting system. However, reaching consensus can be time-consuming, potentially slowing down the development process. Furthermore, the risk of groupthink, where differing opinions are suppressed, needs to be actively mitigated through establishing clear communication protocols and encouraging dissenting voices.

The meritocratic model focuses on rewarding contributions and expertise. Individuals gain influence based on their demonstrated skills and active participation. This encourages high-quality contributions and attracts talented individuals who want to make a meaningful impact. However, this system requires robust mechanisms for evaluating contributions objectively, which can be challenging, particularly in projects with diverse skill sets. Clear, well-defined metrics and transparent review processes are critical for fairness and preventing bias.

Hybrid models combine elements of different approaches, tailored to the specific needs of the project. For instance, a project might use a benevolent dictator for core technical decisions while relying on a community council for broader strategic direction or community management. This flexibility allows projects to adapt their governance structures as they evolve and their needs change. However, designing a hybrid model requires careful planning and clear demarcation of responsibilities to prevent conflicts or ambiguities. It needs well-defined parameters outlining the scope of authority for each governing body.

No matter which model is adopted, open communication is paramount.

Regular updates, transparent decision-making processes, and readily accessible information are essential for building trust and fostering community engagement. Utilizing platforms like mailing lists, forums, or issue trackers allows for open dialogue and ensures everyone has a voice. This open communication, alongside active efforts to nurture a supportive and inclusive environment, is crucial to creating a healthy and sustainable community. Without it, the chosen governance model, no matter how well-designed, may not be enough to ensure long-term success.

Regardless of the chosen model, establishing clear guidelines and procedures is vital. This includes defining roles and responsibilities, outlining the decision-making process, and establishing mechanisms for conflict resolution. Documenting these procedures in a publicly accessible governance document ensures accountability and provides a framework for consistent decision-making. Regular reviews of this document, potentially involving community feedback, are essential to ensure its continued relevance and effectiveness. This fosters transparency, accountability and adaptability within the governance structure itself.

Finally, successful governance relies heavily on community engagement. Active participation from members is essential, not just in making decisions, but also in shaping the project's direction and ensuring its long-term viability. Regular community meetings, surveys, and feedback mechanisms allow members to voice their opinions, contribute to decision-making, and feel a sense of ownership. This cultivates a vibrant and engaged community, ultimately enhancing the project's stability and success. It's about creating a shared vision and a collaborative environment where everyone feels valued and empowered to contribute.

6 Commercial Implications

The commercial landscape surrounding open-source software is surprisingly diverse. It's not simply a matter of giving away your software for free and hoping for the best; successful monetization requires a well-defined strategy. Many companies thrive by offering services around their open-source projects, providing support, training, and customization to clients. This model leverages the free accessibility of the core software, transforming it into a powerful tool for generating recurring revenue. Think of it as building a vibrant ecosystem around your product, rather than simply selling the product itself. The open-source nature fosters community engagement, resulting in invaluable feedback, bug fixes, and feature enhancements – all significantly reducing development costs.

A different approach involves creating a dual licensing model. This strategy involves offering the same software under two distinct licenses: one open-source license for free use and another commercial license for organizations that require additional features, support, or specialized customization beyond what the open-source version offers. This model caters to a wider audience, attracting both individual users and large enterprises. It allows you to balance the benefits of community-driven development with the need for commercial viability. Companies like Redis Labs have successfully employed this approach, demonstrating its effectiveness. Careful consideration of pricing and feature differentiation is crucial, however, to avoid undermining the open-source offering.

Another compelling strategy is to focus on selling premium support and maintenance packages. Even with freely available software, users often value reliable support and timely updates. Offering different tiers of support, ranging from basic troubleshooting to dedicated on-site assistance, allows you to generate recurring revenue streams while maintaining the open-source nature of the core product. This approach effectively transforms the support service itself into a valuable product, appealing to users willing to pay for peace of mind and operational stability. The key here is offering a range of options to accommodate varying user needs and budgets.

Beyond direct sales, some companies create a strong business model by selling complementary products and services alongside their open-source software. This could involve developing proprietary tools or extensions that integrate seamlessly with the open-source software, providing additional functionality or improved performance. For example, a company could offer a comprehensive suite of tools built specifically for managing and optimizing its open-source database, further enhancing its value proposition. This approach can generate significant revenue while remaining consistent with the principles of open-source development. Such a model should be carefully planned to ensure that both the open-source base and the proprietary add-ons complement each other, creating a synergistic whole.

Finally, it's crucial to understand that the choice of open-source license significantly impacts the potential commercial models available. A restrictive license like the GPL may limit the ability to sell proprietary extensions or complementary services, whereas a permissive license like the MIT license offers greater flexibility. Careful consideration of the licensing implications is therefore paramount before launching a commercial venture based on open-source software. A deep understanding of the legal landscape surrounding open-source licenses is necessary to avoid potential pitfalls and legal disputes, ensuring a sustainable and profitable enterprise. The right license facilitates a commercial model that resonates with both the open-source ethos and the demands of the marketplace, creating a powerful synergy between community contributions and profitable enterprise. Choosing wisely means aligning your business model with your chosen license to maximize your chances of success. This is far more than just a technical consideration; it's a fundamental business decision with lasting implications. Get expert legal advice; don't just rely on your gut feeling.

6.1 Open Source Business Models

Many successful businesses thrive on open-source software, yet generating revenue from freely available code demands creative strategies. One prominent model is the dual licensing approach. This involves offering the software under a permissive license like the MIT License for general use, and a separate, commercially-licensed version with added features, support, or specialized integrations. This caters to both individual users and corporations seeking premium services, thereby creating multiple income streams. Think of it as offering a free, basic product and a more advanced, paid version—a common business practice adapted to the open-source world. Successfully implementing this requires careful consideration of feature differentiation to justify the premium price. The additional services must offer compelling value beyond the basic free offering.

A contrasting strategy revolves around offering support and services for open-source projects. Companies can generate revenue by providing training, consulting, customization, and ongoing maintenance for open-source software. This is particularly effective with widely adopted projects where users require expert assistance to integrate the software into their systems or overcome technical hurdles. This approach requires a deep understanding of the target audience's needs and possessing skilled personnel capable of providing high-quality support. Investing in robust documentation and creating accessible community forums can enhance this model, fostering a positive user experience and encouraging further support contracts.

Another way to profit from open-source software is through the sale of related products and services. This encompasses hardware that integrates seamlessly with open-source software, specialized add-ons that

enhance functionalities, or even training courses and certifications that educate users on optimizing the software's use. This approach leverages the software's popularity to sell complementary goods and services. It's a less direct monetization strategy but can create a significant revenue stream, especially when the open-source software becomes a cornerstone of a larger ecosystem. A key to success lies in understanding the users' needs and crafting products that effectively address them. The subscription model offers a recurring revenue stream, especially relevant for sophisticated open-source solutions. This model provides access to premium features, exclusive support, or regular updates for a recurring fee. It encourages long-term relationships with clients, creating a predictable income flow. The subscription model's effectiveness relies heavily on consistently delivering value through continuous improvements, new features, and reliable support. This model is ideal for software that requires ongoing maintenance and updates, providing strong incentives for the company to invest in improvement.
Finally, for those with a strong developer community, a venture capital-backed approach can be considered. While not strictly a business model in itself, it can provide funding for further open-source development and allows for future monetization through other methods. Building a large, engaged community around your software significantly boosts its appeal to investors. A strong community demonstrates user interest and indicates future potential for commercial success, making it more attractive to venture capitalists. This approach requires a well-defined roadmap to success, showing potential for growth and sustainable revenue generation, not just immediate profits.

6.2 Monetizing Open Source

Many successful businesses thrive on open-source software. However, the seemingly altruistic nature of open source can present a challenge: how do you make money from something freely available? This isn't an insurmountable hurdle; it's a solvable problem with various proven strategies. The key is understanding your market and offering value beyond the core open-source offering.

One effective approach involves providing commercial support for your open-source project. Imagine releasing a powerful, free tool, then offering premium support packages – think priority bug fixes, dedicated technical assistance, and customized training. This tiered system attracts users who value quick resolutions and expert guidance. The open-source project serves as a powerful marketing tool, attracting potential paying customers who have already experienced the product's capabilities firsthand. Businesses like Red Hat have built empires on this model, offering robust support and services around a core of free open-source software.

Another route involves creating proprietary extensions or add-ons for your open-source project. This allows you to offer enhanced functionality or specialized features that aren't included in the free version. Think of it as building a solid foundation with open-source and then creating lucrative add-ons that cater to specific needs or integrate with other systems. This strategy effectively leverages the open-source community's contributions while creating a sustainable revenue stream from premium features. The open-source base attracts users, and the paid add-ons cater to those requiring more advanced functionalities.

Consider focusing on specialized services. Rather than directly monetizing the software itself, you could offer professional services related to its implementation, customization, or integration into existing systems. This works particularly well with complex open-source projects that require expertise to configure or deploy effectively. Your value lies not in the software itself, but in the knowledge and skills you possess to help businesses seamlessly incorporate that software into their operations. A strong understanding of the open-source project becomes your competitive edge.

Don't underestimate the power of training and consulting. Offering workshops, webinars, or one-on-one consulting services can be a lucrative way to monetize your expertise. Your deep understanding of the open-source project positions you as a valuable resource for businesses and individuals looking to maximize its potential. This directly translates into a profitable service, particularly if your expertise is in high demand within a niche market. Creating high-quality educational content can also serve as a marketing tool, generating leads for your consulting services.

Finally, building a strong community around your open-source project can indirectly lead to monetization opportunities. A thriving community fosters a positive image, draws in more users, and may even attract potential investors or partners who see the value in supporting the project's growth. Community management skills are key here; fostering collaboration and providing avenues for user contributions can create a sense of ownership and loyalty that translates into financial success. The community itself can organically contribute to the project's value and expand its potential for monetization.

The key to successfully monetizing open-source projects lies in strategic thinking and a keen understanding of user needs. It's not about abandoning the philosophy of open source; it's about finding innovative and sustainable ways to support its development and expansion while also generating revenue. Many paths exist. Carefully consider the unique characteristics of your open-source project and your target market to find the best strategy for your success. Remember, open-source doesn't mean "free to make money from"; it means "free to use," leaving many avenues for generating revenue. The focus should be on adding value, not exploiting a free resource; providing solutions and services around it rather than the software itself often yields the greatest rewards.

7 Future of Open Source Licensing

The increasing integration of AI and machine learning into software development presents a significant challenge and opportunity for open-source licensing. Existing licenses may struggle to adequately address the complexities of AI-generated code, which blurs traditional notions of authorship and copyright. We might see the emergence of new licensing models specifically designed for AI-assisted development, perhaps incorporating clauses related to data usage, model training, and potential biases in algorithms. This necessitates a deeper engagement with legal and ethical considerations to ensure fairness, transparency, and accountability. The legal landscape will need to adapt to a world where software creation is increasingly collaborative between humans and machines.

Adapting open-source licenses to the era of the metaverse poses another intriguing challenge. As open-source software finds increasing application in virtual and augmented reality environments, the traditional concepts of distribution and access need to be re-evaluated. Licensing may need to incorporate clauses addressing the unique aspects of 3D assets, virtual worlds, and user-generated content within these spaces. This also raises questions about the ownership and licensing of data generated within metaverse applications built using open-source components. Developing robust, adaptable licensing frameworks for this rapidly evolving digital environment is crucial for continued innovation.

Another critical aspect of the future of open-source licensing is the growing emphasis on security and privacy. As software becomes increasingly intertwined with sensitive personal data, the need for clear and comprehensive licensing terms addressing security vulnerabilities and data protection becomes paramount. We can expect a surge in licenses that explicitly incorporate security considerations, perhaps requiring developers to address identified vulnerabilities promptly, and implement rigorous security auditing procedures. This will undoubtedly place additional responsibilities on developers but ultimately benefit end-users by improving the overall security posture of open-source applications.

The rise of copyleft licenses, which require derivative works to also be released under the same or a compatible license, has fostered a significant ecosystem of collaborative development. However, concerns remain about their potential to restrict innovation or create barriers to entry for smaller contributors. The future may see a more nuanced approach, with a greater emphasis on flexibility and a wider range of license options tailored to different project needs. This might include variations of copyleft licenses that allow for more limited commercial use or integration into proprietary systems. The balance between promoting collaboration and fostering innovation remains a key challenge.

Finally, the future of open-source licensing is inextricably linked to the evolution of open-source communities themselves. Strong, well-governed communities are essential for maintaining the quality, security, and ethical standards of open-source software. We can anticipate increased investment in community building initiatives, with a focus on fostering inclusive participation, improving communication, and establishing robust dispute resolution mechanisms. The future of open source is not simply about the licenses themselves, but also the collaborative ecosystems that support them. Supporting these communities through effective governance and clear licensing frameworks will be key to ensuring the ongoing success and sustainability of open-source software development. The increasing importance of community-based governance and conflict resolution mechanisms is also important to note. It's crucial to encourage participation and transparency to build robust and sustainable open-source projects.

7.1 Emerging Trends

The rise of copyleft licenses, particularly those with strong viral effects like the GPL, is slowing. We're seeing a shift towards more permissive licenses, such as the MIT and Apache 2.0 licenses. This isn't a rejection of open source principles; rather, it reflects a growing need for interoperability and ease of integration in increasingly complex software ecosystems. Businesses are increasingly favoring licenses that allow them greater freedom to incorporate open-source components into their proprietary products without the constraints of copyleft. This pragmatic approach prioritizes practicality over ideological purity, leading to a broader adoption of open-source technologies. The increased collaboration between corporations and open-source projects fuels this trend, with many companies contributing resources and expertise while benefiting from the flexibility of permissive licensing.

Software supply chain security is becoming paramount, and this impacts licensing significantly. Open-source projects are scrutinized more rigorously for vulnerabilities, leading to a demand for more transparent and auditable licensing processes. We are witnessing a rise in tools and techniques designed to help developers and users verify the authenticity and integrity of open-source components, including automated license scanning and compliance checks. This heightened awareness is driving a more proactive approach to security within the open-source community and is reshaping how licenses are designed and implemented to guarantee better security and transparency for all stakeholders. It's not just about the code anymore; it's about the entire chain of custody and the provenance of every single piece of software.

The emergence of AI and machine learning technologies profoundly influences open-source licensing. AI models are increasingly trained on vast datasets, often incorporating open-source code and data. The legal implications of training AI on copyrighted material or data subject to open-source licenses are still being explored. Questions arise regarding the ownership of models generated by AI trained on open-source data and the appropriate attribution. Clearer guidelines and best practices are needed to navigate the complex intersection of AI, copyright, and open-source licensing, potentially requiring new licensing models that specifically address the unique challenges of AI development. The legal landscape is adapting slowly but surely, grappling with the revolutionary changes introduced by AI.

The expansion of the Internet of Things (IoT) presents new licensing challenges. The sheer volume and diversity of devices in the IoT ecosystem necessitate simplified and adaptable licensing mechanisms. Traditional open-source licenses may be too complex or cumbersome for the resource-constrained environments typical of IoT devices. This is leading to the exploration of alternative licensing models that balance the benefits of openness with the practical limitations of embedded systems. These models must be tailored to the specific requirements of IoT devices, taking into account their limited processing power, memory, and connectivity. This situation requires a reevaluation of existing open-source practices to adequately address the novel circumstances of the growing IoT sector.

Finally, there's an increasing focus on the ethical aspects of open-source licensing. Discussions regarding equitable access to technology, the responsible use of open-source software, and the potential for exploitation are gaining prominence. The open-source community is actively working towards creating more inclusive and sustainable practices, fostering collaboration and promoting responsible innovation. This includes efforts to improve the diversity and inclusivity of the open-source community and to address issues such as bias in algorithms and data. Ethical considerations are moving from the margins to the center of discussions surrounding open-source software. It's no longer enough to simply develop and distribute code; the ethical implications of that distribution must also be addressed thoughtfully and proactively. The future of open source depends not only on its technological advancements but also on its ability to uphold strong ethical standards.

7.2 Challenges and Opportunities

The rapid evolution of open-source software presents both significant challenges and exciting opportunities. Navigating this landscape requires a keen understanding of the evolving legal and ethical considerations, alongside the ever-shifting dynamics of community involvement and commercial exploitation. Failing to adapt to these changes can lead to legal entanglements, missed opportunities, and ultimately, the stifling of innovation. Conversely, embracing the opportunities can unlock unprecedented levels of collaboration and economic growth.

One pressing challenge is the increasing complexity of open-source licenses. While the core principles remain consistent, the nuances of specific license terms have become increasingly intricate, requiring specialized legal expertise for proper interpretation and compliance. This complexity can deter smaller developers and businesses, potentially hindering the broader adoption of open-source solutions. This raises significant barriers to entry, particularly for those lacking access to legal counsel. The lack of uniform interpretation across jurisdictions adds another layer of difficulty, making it imperative to carefully consider the global implications of license choices.

However, this complexity also opens up opportunities for innovative business models. Specialized services focused on license compliance and consultation represent a burgeoning market. Companies can thrive by offering tailored solutions to help organizations navigate the intricacies of open-source licensing, ensuring legal compliance while maximizing the benefits of open-source technologies. This creates a niche for experienced professionals capable of translating legal complexities into practical, actionable advice for businesses of all sizes. This expertise becomes particularly critical as open-source software continues its integration into more complex systems.

Another significant challenge arises from the evolving nature of open-source communities. While community involvement is fundamental to the success of many projects, managing diverse perspectives and ensuring equitable contributions can be difficult. Maintaining a healthy, productive community requires skilled leadership, effective communication strategies, and clear governance structures. Disputes over project direction, contributions, or even the very core philosophy of the project can arise and disrupt development.

Despite these challenges, the vibrancy and inclusivity of open-source communities offer immense opportunities. They foster a collaborative environment that brings together diverse talent from around the world, accelerating innovation and knowledge sharing. This global collaboration facilitates the development of sophisticated, high-quality software, benefiting users worldwide. Furthermore, the open nature of these communities promotes transparency and accountability, fostering trust and credibility. By actively participating in and nurturing these communities, individuals and organizations can gain valuable skills, build professional networks, and contribute to projects that address global challenges.

The commercialization of open-source software presents both challenges and opportunities. While monetizing open-source projects can be challenging, it is far from impossible. Successful models involve a shift in perspective, moving away from traditional proprietary licensing toward innovative strategies that leverage the open nature of the software. This could include offering support services, consulting, training, or creating value-added products and services that integrate with or extend the core open-source offering. Companies that successfully navigate this transition often find themselves with a sustainable and highly scalable business model.

The challenges related to intellectual property rights remain a critical hurdle. Understanding copyright, patent, and trademark implications within the open-source context is essential to avoid legal pitfalls. Clear attribution, proper license selection, and due diligence in utilizing third-party components are all crucial aspects to consider. The potential for disputes involving intellectual property rights highlights the need for legal expertise and careful planning throughout the software development lifecycle. However, navigating these legal complexities also creates opportunities for lawyers, consultants, and compliance specialists.

Despite the inherent challenges, the future of open-source licensing is bright. The continued growth of open-source software underscores its critical role in technological innovation. By proactively addressing the challenges related to license complexity, community management, and commercialization, we can unlock the immense potential of open-source software to foster collaboration, drive innovation, and benefit society as a whole. The opportunities are vast, requiring proactive engagement, strategic planning, and a willingness to embrace change. Successfully navigating these complexities will lead to significant growth and innovation within the open-source ecosystem.

7.3 Ethical Considerations

Open source thrives on collaboration, but ethical considerations are paramount. The very nature of shared code necessitates a careful examination of responsibility. We aren't simply sharing files; we're sharing the building blocks of future innovations, and this sharing demands a high level of integrity.

Transparency is a cornerstone of the open-source philosophy, yet even the most transparent project can suffer ethical lapses. Consider the implications of intentionally omitting crucial security vulnerabilities within your code, or knowingly using code snippets from elsewhere without proper attribution. These actions, while potentially hidden in the vastness of an open-source project, erode the trust and collaboration upon which the entire ecosystem depends. Each line of code carries a burden of responsibility; it's not just data, it's a statement about our ethical commitment to the community.

The ease of contribution, however, presents both opportunities and risks. While readily available code simplifies development, it also increases the risk of inadvertently incorporating flawed or malicious code. This emphasizes the vital importance of thorough code review and testing, not merely as a technical necessity, but as an ethical duty to the users who will depend upon the software. Consider the downstream effects of a poorly-vetted component; this isn't just a matter of fixing a bug, but protecting users from potentially serious consequences. Responsible development includes robust testing and code review procedures, designed to mitigate both intentional and unintentional harms. Contributing to open source isn't just about writing code; it's about participating in a community. Respectful communication, constructive criticism, and fair collaboration are critical. Think of the impact of aggressive behavior, personal attacks, or the silencing of dissenting voices. Such actions undermine the very collaborative spirit that makes open source possible. A healthy open-source community fosters growth and innovation, while a toxic one stifles progress. Our ethical responsibility extends beyond the code itself, encompassing how we interact and engage with fellow developers and users.

Moreover, the licensing aspect presents significant ethical dimensions. While legal compliance is essential, the ethical implications go beyond mere legality. Selecting a license that adequately protects the rights of contributors while allowing for broad use requires careful consideration. Ignoring or misinterpreting license terms can cause significant harm, not just legally, but to the entire community. Choosing a license is a commitment – a promise to uphold the terms and respect the intellectual property rights involved. This commitment isn't a mere formality, it represents an ethical pledge to the entire open-source ecosystem. Commercial aspects of open source also introduce a complex ethical landscape. Monetizing open-source projects is perfectly acceptable; indeed, it can be vital for supporting long-term development and sustainability. However, ethical concerns arise when monetization strategies prioritize profit over community benefit. Exploiting open-source components without reciprocal contributions, or engaging in deceptive practices around open-source models, are clearly unethical behaviors. The open-source community depends on fair play and collaborative partnerships, fostering an environment that values both commercial success and communal welfare. A responsible approach balances these two vital components.

Ultimately, ethical considerations in open source are not merely about adhering to a code of conduct, but about fostering a community of trust, integrity, and mutual respect. Each participant plays a critical role in shaping the overall ethical landscape. By embracing transparent practices, engaging in responsible development, participating constructively in communities, carefully selecting and complying with licenses, and applying fair commercial principles, we can build a more ethical and sustainable future for open source software. The future of open-source hinges on our collective ethical responsibility.

www.ingramcontent.com/pod-product-compliance
Ingram Content Group UK Ltd.
Pitfield, Milton Keynes, MK11 3LW, UK
UKHW020155290926
15471UKWH00005B/885

9 798349 376061